A MEMOIR IN POETRY

I LOVED YOU IN *Paris*

JULIETTE *Sobanet*

I0111596

Saint Germain
press

San Diego, California

Cover design, interior book design,
and eBook design
by Blue Harvest Creative
www.blueharvestcreative.com

Author photography by Carl Israelsson

Published by
Saint Germain Press

Library of Congress Control Number:
2016933666

ISBN-13: 978-0692644256
ISBN-10: 0692644253

Visit the author at her website:
www.juliettesobanet.com
and *www.bhcauthors.com*

Visit Juliette's website by scanning the QR code.

For Tim
who found solace in writing
beautiful strings
of words
~ and ~
for my mom
who has always
praised me
for mine

TABLE OF CONTENTS

UN PETIT MOT DE L'AUTEUR ~
A NOTE FROM THE AUTHOR

We all have stories inside of us, stories that swirl around us and through us, stories that dance in our hearts and need to come out. Whether they're fictional or true, these stories we all tell shed light on our universal experience as humans to love, to lose, to create new life, and if we're brave enough, to love again. It's a never ending cycle, one that we can all relate to, and one that we all need help surviving. Writing the poems in this book helped me to survive and make sense of some of the darkest days of my life, to love even deeper, and to embrace the new life I've created and all of the happiness and heartache that entails. Writing these poems has led me to the place where I am now—a place of joy, freedom, and a total gratitude for life. Much of that gratitude goes to you, my readers, for taking this journey with me first in my memoir, *Meet Me in Paris*, and now through this collection of poetry. While my choices may not reflect your own, I'm sure you have loved. I'm sure you have lost. And I'm sure you have needed help to weather the storms that have whipped through the story of your own wild, beautiful life. So, human to human, soul to soul, we aren't that different at all. We all tell a story that ultimately, every time, goes back to love. It is with this love that I share my words, my truth, and my own wild, beautiful story with you.

Love,
Juliette

Partie I

UNE MAÎTRESSE ET SON AMANT
~ A MISTRESS AND HER LOVER ~

THE BEGINNING

I was hungry
When I first saw you
Broken, fragile
Thirsty, in need

My eyes
They fled to you
Bled through the air
Seeped into your pores
Took possession

In an instant
I belonged
Only to you

Even from across the room
I was chained to you
My heart, yours for the taking

My soul fell hard, fast
Into your smooth hands
Trapped within your savage desire
A wildfire burning in every cell

You didn't even know
You had yet to touch me

But I was already
Irreversibly, forever
Yours

DID MY SOUL ALREADY KNOW?

Did my soul already know?
Had she already planned that magical night?
The night your eyes would take me hostage
The night chemistry would flow between us, effortlessly
An electric current of heat

My soul, she must have known
How important you would become to me
How happy I would be
Knowing you exist

She knew...that smart, vibrant, sexy soul
She totally knew

You are a gift
A beautiful, perfectly timed gift
One I will never take for granted
One I will love, always, for this
For where you have taken me

The world has opened
Now that you have arrived

EVEN BEFORE

I loved you even before
Those wings
Whisked your hungry heart
Through the heavens
Across an ocean
Into my arms

You knew this, of course
When a photograph
Of my lustful skin
Stained your inbox

Intoxicated, you became
Not from the sting of the alcohol
But from the way the light
Kissed my fallen hair

That morning
My heart may have burst
Had you not
Stepped off the plane

But you saved
My wounded mesh
Of flesh and ribs
And blood and tears
From a sudden
And tragic
Death

Your smile so luminous
The heavens had to squint

But my eyes grew to the size
Of a blue moon shining
Over the magnificent city
We would soon paint
With our love
Our sex
Our fire
Our tears

I loved you even before
Those wings
Whisked you away
From a wife
Who didn't know

That across an ocean
Her love would be tested

In the arms of a mistress
Who was falling
Who was stealing
The hungry heart
Of her husband

ON YOUR BIRTHDAY...

I want you to know
That of all the souls
Who have crossed paths with mine
I am happiest to have found yours

I want you to know
That wherever you go
Wherever I go
I will always think of you

I want you to know
That you have brought to my life
A bliss, a fever, a dance, a desire
I've never known before

I want you to know
That for me, you are
More than a body
More than a lover
More than your handsome smile
Or your sexy boy band hair

For me
You are a connection, an arrow
Straight to my heart
Into my soul

I want you to know
That my soul was waiting for you
And when she found you
She breathed a sigh of relief...
You do exist, after all

On your birthday, lover
I want you to know
That I am forever grateful
Forever filled
With desire, passion, and joy
Just to know you

And whatever happens
Whether our paths stay
On this same intense journey together...
Or veer far away from one another

I will always feel
Your heat, your warmth
Your sweet, adoring smile
Right next to me

I want you to know, too
That I would follow you to the ends of the earth...
Or to a motel in the middle of Kansas
I don't care, really

It's you I want
Plain and simple
It's you

Happy Birthday, lover

THE IN-BETWEEN

I am in the in-between

In love
Total, relentless, all-consuming love

But protecting myself
From the way
You shatter my heart

Every sunrise
Every sunset
And every moment in between

Is it an illusion?
To think we could have a happy ending
To think that one day
You will choose me

Am I crazy?
Straddling this line

Some days I am sure
Absolutely certain
You will come to me
Only me

And other days
I am
Tormented, tortured, heartbroken

Because you are far
So far away

That is my reality
You are not here

I am alone
And in love

A most intoxicating love

Which keeps me in between
Love and sanity
Joy and heartbreak
Reality and illusion

Which will it be, lover?

THE LOST PUZZLE PIECE

What if you came to me tonight?
Told me it was forever
That you'd never leave us
That you'd love me, only me
For all of time

Tonight I am alone
A solo survivor on this starry canyon
Thousands of miles from your smooth hands
And the lost puzzle piece of your body

ONE MORE LOVE LETTER

Tonight, my lover
I want to write you one more love letter
Just to tell you
How deeply I adore you

How you are on my mind
Every sunrise, every sunset
And on every star in between
I wish for you
Only you
Always you

If you were here, beside me tonight
I would show you how much I love you
How my desire for your lips is stronger
Than the moon's pull on the tide

How I never want to have you as far as those stars
How, if I could, I would hold your hands
Whisk away all of your troubles
And make you smile, endlessly, forever

If you came to me, tonight
I would give you every star in the sky
Every sunrise
Every sunset
And every heartbeat in between

They're all for you, lover...
Only you

ON THE STREETS OF NEW ORLEANS

The south buzzes around us
Yellow and pink houses
Porches with swings and strings of light
Your eyes, the way they love me

I've never seen anything so beautiful

You tilt your head, sweeter than tea
Smiling at me, talking about our island wedding
You wouldn't marry me, you ask
As you suck down a slimy oyster

Me, in my polka dot dress, lavender scarf
A country girl for the night
Simple
And in love

I wouldn't marry anyone else, I say
But you...yes, I would marry you

Summer has yet to arrive this night
As we stroll over broken sidewalks
Wishing these perfect homes were our own

My heart stumbles, dives, lands at our feet
Because we hold hands
Knowing this is the end

Once again
Clumsy, clutching, wishing
This heart of mine
She hasn't learned

In the cab ride home
I turn my face away
Tears flood my lashes

You are the one I love
The one I dreamt of, searched for, found...
The one I am losing

You love me
Still you go back to her

I am a passing love
Wishing I could be more
Hoping that someday I will be

Because for me
You are the stars, the moon, my entire universe
I would give away all the light in the sky
For you, only you

That night in New Orleans
I wonder if the children asleep in their beds
Awoke to the sound of shattering

Or if the cats roaming the streets
Hungry, prowling, howling...
I wonder if they heard it too

My heart, smashed to pieces
On the streets of New Orleans

A FATAL OFFERING

My heart needed the assurance of death
And that is what your love offered
Death, in its purest form
A broken heart will always kill you

It killed me
Again
And again
And again

Who will come along
And give my heart refuge
From this violent storm
This series of deaths

I want life again
I want love again

And so, I will believe
I will hope
I will pray

And I will love you
With my wounded heart
Forever

I AM WORTH MORE

I am worth more than a quick hello
I am worth more than a secret rendezvous
I am worth more than "if," than "one day," than "hopefully"

I am worth more than the spare time
In between your meetings
And your phone calls to your wife

I am worth more than a vehicle for sex
Than a pretty girl who dances
Who you must hide in a hotel room

I am worth more than your words

I am worth action
I am worth true love
And I will accept nothing less in my life

I deserve the whole package

And that is why I'm leaving you

ONE ENDLESS MOMENT

What if this
Me, you, us
Our intoxicating love
Was all a plan
Orchestrated by our sweet souls
In one endless moment
As we swam in the abyss of eternal twilight

Shimmering, glowing, loving
We shook hearts
Intertwined souls
Yours indigo and mine violet
Streaking across a starry sky
Our cosmic connection
Sealed
In one endless night

Gazing down at this wild world
We would soon enter
In a fit of screams
Knowing we wouldn't remember
The agreement we made
As souls, with only the intention
Of learning
Of growth

We knew it would hurt
Like hell
But the wisdom we held between lives
Insisted the love would be worth the pain

And it took me a while, here
In this string of moments
That one day
Will end
But I know now
You were worth the darkness
Your shadows brighter still
Than the most blinding star
In that trippy cosmos we painted
With our infinity

Someday the dust
Will reclaim these two bodies
That once intertwined
In fits of ecstasy
In hotel beds all over this world
But our sweet souls
Yours electric indigo, and mine a lustrous violet
Will dance in eternal bliss
Until we are ready
To plummet into the jungle
And do it all again...

Next time, I wonder
Will our connection break my heart
So thoroughly
Or will our love, perhaps
Be grounded in something more solid
Than a married man
And his mistress

Whatever it will be
We wrote our love in the stars
I dreamed you
And you dreamed me
Lovers, eternal

And so, forever it will be
In one endless, brilliant moment

Partie II

Une femme et son mari
~ A wife and her husband ~

HOW?

It is in the worst of times
When we discover who we truly are
What we are made of

We are weak, all of us
We want something firm, something strong to hold onto
I don't want to be alone
I never have

But you weren't there, when I needed you
You couldn't meet me where I was at

We failed, we both failed
I never wanted it to turn out this way
I didn't marry you thinking this would happen
That I would have to leave you to survive
That I would feel like part of my soul, half of my heart
Had been ripped, torn, shred to pieces
After you left
After I got what I wanted
What I thought I wanted

Now I am here
Alone
Lost
Wishing you were here

But not you
The you I wanted you to be
The you I always hoped you would be
The you who you never became
The you who you will never be

You'll never be him
And I'll never be her

But we did love each other
I did love you
I still do, and I always will

Which is why my heart is broken
Totally, utterly, desperately broken

I am so sorry I couldn't be what you needed
That you couldn't be what I needed

I'm sorry I fell in love with someone else
Someone who can't be with me

Karma, right?
A sick twist of fate

Will I ever smile again?
I don't know
I honestly don't know

I can only hope
I can only believe in a better time
A better life

The life I hoped for when I told you
I couldn't be with you anymore

But now, sitting here in our home, without you
I wonder what I have done
What on earth was I thinking
When I told you I was leaving you?

How will I survive this?
How will I get through the day?
The week?
The month?

How will I write?
I don't have the energy to dance, the creativity to write

I am zapped, exhausted, tapped out

I am limp, desolate, alone

And I just want to be happy
I want something strong to hold onto

Once you were my life vest
Together we became a sinking ship

I jumped off to swim to sunnier skies, safer shores

But I am stranded in the middle of the ocean
The waves are crashing over me
And I don't know if I will ever breathe again

IF I GO

If I go, I want you to know
How much light you brought to my life
How I loved you
More than I loved myself

Which is why I'm here
On my knees
In despair
The darkest darkness
A night with no stars

Except I know the stars are there
Waiting for me
They are my home
And I am ready to go

Will you stand by me
When I have lost everything
When I have nothing left to give
When I am no more
Than the tears streaming down my face

Because I have stood there, by you
By all of you
In the worst of times
Yet I am here
Alone

A father who never wanted me
A mother who doesn't believe I love her
A husband who couldn't grow with me
A lover who hides me in the shadows

So where does that leave me?

My friends are my true family, my love, my rock
Thank you, friends, for being there

If I go, you should know
That I'm not leaving because of you
I'm leaving because there was nowhere left for me to go

And I love you
Each and every one of you

The father who never wanted me
The mother who doesn't believe I love her
The husband who couldn't grow with me
The lover who hides me in the shadows
And my friends, my dear sweet friends

I love you
Every single one of you
And when I am gone, I will continue loving you

THE NEXT TIME

The next time a friend tells you she is getting a divorce...

Act as if she has just told you
That the dearest person in her life
The person she has loved for sunrises and sunsets
For starry nights and stormy skies
And every moment in between

Act as if she has just told you that this person has died...

Because that is what has happened.

The next time a friend tells you she is getting a divorce...

Act as if she has just told you
That the dearest person in her life
The person who has loved her at her best and at her worst
Who has held her up and torn her down
Who has been her everything for too many days to count

Act as if she has just told you that this person has died...

Because that is what has happened.

The next time a friend tells you she is getting a divorce...

Act as if she has just told you
That the relationship she thought would last forever
The relationship that sustained her
Filled her up
Tore her down

Act as if she has just told you
That this relationship has died...

Because that is what has happened.

The next time a friend tells you she is getting a divorce...

Act as if she has just told you that she is about to enter
The most intense grieving period of her life
And that a part of her has died too

Because that is what has happened.

The next time a friend tells you she is getting a divorce...

Know that she will need your support
More than she will ever admit
And even if she smiles and says she is okay
Please know that underneath that smile
Your friend is suffering
Your friend is drowning in loss
Your friend needs your help

Because she is grieving a death
A death she may have chosen
A death he may have chosen
But it is a death, nonetheless

The next time a friend tells you she is getting a divorce...

Know that it may take years for her to feel better
It may take years for her to feel joy every day
Know that she will be so tired of this grief
That she will try to hide it

But it is still there
And she needs your help

The next time a friend tells you she is getting a divorce...

Know that depression may set in
And depression is a beast
It's a killer
And when she reaches out to you
You must go to her
Drop your plans
Get in the car or hop on a plane
And *go*

Go again, and again, and again
Because she needs you
Even if she doesn't want to admit it

Because there are days when she doesn't want to live
Even if she doesn't want to admit it

And because one day
You will lose someone you loved
More than you loved yourself
Whether through a divorce
A death
Or both

And you will need her too

The next time a friend tells you she is getting a divorce...

The best thing you can do is hold a space for her to grieve
Without telling her why her life is so fabulous
And why she should feel good

The best thing you can do is hold her
And let her cry
Until the storm passes

The best thing you can do is be there for her
Always and forever
No matter what

YOUR SONG

I hear your song
Everywhere I go

I remember the feeling of you

Your essence
Your smile
Your touch

Everyday life
Is a ghost town
Of you, my love

The man I've loved for so long
The man I left
The man I thought I could let go

But that was idiotic
To think I could ever
Cut the ties that bind us

Those ropes
They were worn
Thinning
Nearly invisible
When I told you
I had to go

But what I discovered
After I left

Was an invisible rope
Splashed with your blood
And mine
Tied to my core
Tied to yours

And it will
Never
Ever
Be Broken

AND YOU

Last night I dreamt of coffins and hurricanes
And you
This morning while lying on my back
I called in the angels
To take away
The heaviness, the weight, the darkness
In my chest
That the coffins and the hurricanes
And you
Left in your wake

Thankfully my angels never tire
For I do
So often
When I dream of coffins
And hurricanes
And you

A HEART FOREVER TORN

The other day I thought of you
I thought of our divorce
I remembered the way
I used to make you laugh
When I would pretend to cry
And the way you used to make me smile
When you danced in the kitchen

Even though the laughing stopped
Even though the dancing stopped
Even though that thing we used to have
Died

I cried for us

And I knew
In that broken heart of mine
That no matter where you are
No matter where I am
I will always love you
I will always wish I had never left
I will always be thankful I left

Opposites that create
A heart forever torn

I wonder if my blood has reached you
Laced into your veins in the night
Even though a new love
Sleeps by your side

I wonder if you dream of me
On the same cold nights
When my mind travels to you

If I had been able to see the future
I would have tried harder
I would have given more warning
There are a million things I would have done
And would not have done

We may have still ended up
In a heap of broken promises
And salty tears

But perhaps
There would have been a different ending
To our beautiful love story
An ending without an ending
An eternity of knowing
We would always have each other
Until death swept one
Or both
Of our hopeless souls
Into an abyss of love

Instead
My impulsiveness
My unhappiness
My sadness
Insisted
On breaking the one thing
I wish
Had never broken

The other day I thought of you
I thought of our divorce
The best
The worst
Decision

The consequences of that one choice
Will slice my heart
Until the day
It stops beating

TOGETHER

I saw you again
In my dreams last night
You held me like you knew
You had lost me
I knew I had lost you too

And we were finished
Losing each other
We were back together
Two bodies, two hearts, two souls,
As one relieved bodyheartsoul

It was your face
Your arms
Your body
It was you
When you told me you loved me

But when you began to tell me the story
Of why you never proposed to her
I woke up
And remembered

You did propose
You are married
But not to me
Anymore

You lost me
I lost you

And together
Is only a word
We used to know

I LOVED YOU IN PARIS

I thought this poem would be about him
The one I ran to when I dove
Out of our union
And shattered those beating things
Inside our chests
We used to call hearts

I did love him in Paris
In a secret flat
Of red sheets
And violet couches
And forbidden declarations
The heaven and the hell of adultery

But you
You were the first one I loved in Paris

I always tell people
You would never come
But that's a lie

It was only a weekend
But you and I
We spilled our love
All over those cobblestone streets
Kids who had no clue
What the years would bring

It didn't matter then
When we ate French fries
Beneath the Eiffel Tower

Two American clichés
Raining kisses in a city
Already drenched in love

It didn't matter
When your bright blue eyes
Lit up the skies
And I snapped a photo of you
And that most adoring smile

A photo I've carried everywhere I go
It's still in my room
In an album not far
From the gown that sleeps in a coffin
Preserved, white, sparkling
For no one

I don't have the heart
To look at the picture
Of the day
I loved you in Paris

I thought this poem would be about him
But no
That beating thing
Inside my chest
Only travels one path
A path that always and forever
Leads back to you

THE NIGHT WE MET

Yes, I know
It was in the eighties room
Of a sketchy dance club
When those wounded blue eyes
First found mine

Bright, open, young
Unsuspecting that a simple dance
And a phone number scribbled on a napkin
Would lead to twelve years
In each other's arms

I'm not sure if you know
But that wasn't the first time
Our souls crossed paths

In another world
At a full moon ball
Beneath a twinkling blanket of stars
Your sphere of light found my sphere of light
And what came next
Was a cosmic collision
Sending shock waves throughout the universe
In that moment was created
A forever love

I know this because of the way
You breathe beneath my skin
Rush through my veins
Lodge yourself in my marrow
Almost as if
We are one

And even though
In this temporary life
In this lost world
We are no longer one

Somewhere else
In this vast magnificent universe
You are mine
And I am yours

Still, I am here
I am now
And my sphere of light
Misses your sphere of light

I know this life is fleeting
I believe in the promise of eternity
Of full moon balls
Where we will dance again
All night, in ridiculously orgasmic love

But this doesn't, even a tiny bit
Dull the pain I feel
Every time your heart beats within mine
Or in the moments
When your breath replenishes my lungs

Because even though you live within me
Even though my marrow knows only you
I search the world
Frantic, exhausted, devastated
A heap of despair, holding onto a frayed napkin
A scribbled phone number
A simple dance

As I realize
That your wounded blue eyes
Are gone

THE ROOM

Nestled in our first home
With waves just beyond the tips
Of our young, naïve fingers
There was a cozy little room
A second bedroom, we thought
Or perhaps, an office

But on the day we moved in
I walked its perimeter
Running fingers over smooth white walls
Imagining the day
When we would paint them
In blue or pink splashes of our love
For our baby
A child who had yet to come

Life swooped in, though
Catapulted our hopeless souls on separate journeys
Yours across the world on a ship that nearly swallowed you
Through sandstorms in searing hot deserts awaiting war
And me to the city I love most
A Paris year, becoming who I'd always wanted to be
Miles and miles apart
Barely a phone call to connect us
Our hearts had never been closer

We returned, a year later
A changed husband and his changed wife
To our beach paradise
And to each other's arms

This time, we could almost hear the waves crashing at night
From our little abode on the 101
With the checkered kitchen floor

But you, you were different
That ship, those sandstorms, the threat of war
Turned you into a man
Who was afraid of living, of giving, of loving
Anyone but me
You didn't dance
On the checkered floor anymore
And Paris had changed me too
I wasn't afraid of anything
This girl was ready to live, give, dream big

Even so
With sand between our toes
And passion bursting in our little bedroom
Our love thrived
We didn't need a second room
For the baby who had yet to arrive
We had our love, and that was more than enough

It wasn't meant to be forever
This little home
With the checkered kitchen floor
So off we went
In search of bigger better things

Our journey swept us away
From the healing scent of salt water
From the waves you so loved to surf
Heaved us across deserts and plains
And spit us out in the city that never sleeps

Our wide eyes were quickly zapped
With a relentless fatigue
New York wore us down
Ate at your insides

One night at the kitchen table
That took up half of our Queens apartment
You looked at me with eyes sunken in
Your heart an erratic beat
Happiness was a memory
You were quickly forgetting
I was still holding, grasping onto hope
For brighter days
And I knew
Our love would suffocate
In this tiny box
Where there was barely room for a couch
Let alone a physical manifestation of our love

So I told you
We must go

Back on the road we were
And finally
This tired husband and his hopeful wife
Found a home in the city where we first met
Life had weathered these two hearts, though
No longer were we those two naïve kids
Dancing with abandon
In the underground of the nation's capital

And a baby still seemed far off
Until...

A new home we bought
Had a room
The room
And one day, I woke up
Knowing I was ready
For a family
For a baby
With you, my love

A bit of convincing
And my skeptical husband
Said yes
But my body...
She said no

A firm, clear, loud
Raging
Motherfucking
No!

A year later
After stress tests and heart monitors
After ultrasounds and acupuncture
After bursting cysts and enough tears to fill an ocean
We moved back across this wide country
To a canyon
That would swallow
Our love
Our hope
Our family that would never be born
Our baby who would never come

Years have passed
No longer are we husband and wife
But yesterday, I found myself
Back at our canyon in the pouring rain
My feet carried me beneath the room
We had reserved
For her
For him

But the room
Belongs to someone else now
Not you or I
Or our baby

As tears filled my lashes
Rainbows lit up the sky
Arching over our canyon
And I cried
For the room that would never hold our child
For our arms that would never be graced with our baby
For the life we would never have

When the brilliant streaks of colors
Left the sky gray and cold
I let my heart fill with gratitude
For you
For us
For our love
For the baby who never came
For every lovely, aching, beautiful moment
That I spent with you

I thanked the heavens
For the way you loved me
And for the way I will always love you
It has been exquisite and exquisitely painful, loving you
You are a gift, one I will keep safe in my heart
No matter where life takes us

Finally
I turned away
From our last home
From the room that held my tears
Instead of our newborn baby's

Memories and rain poured down my cheeks
Oceans of regret soaked my hair
Draining down my temples
Igniting my tears

And I said goodbye
To you
To him
To her
To the room

As I left our canyon
My feet carried me beneath a new rainbow
I marched proud, a soldier of our love
Drenched in wounds
Soaked in acceptance
And ever so grateful
For this tragically beautiful dance
We call life
And for my second chance
To create one
Anew

LETTING GO

Lady Moon dangles low
Tonight, just for us
Her orange glow lights my memory of you
Embers of your kisses sparkle, fall at my feet
The stars in your baby blues shoot in crisscross daggers
Across the chilly black sky of my heart

She's so cold without you

A whisper, as our lovely moon
Travels higher in the sky
Let him go, let him go, let him go
She says

I am defiant, though
I will not, I cannot, I don't know how
I've ridden dangerously
On the coattails of time
I've kissed the lips of a million men
But neither time nor the adoration of another
Can steal what has been
And always will be
Yours

My heart, I tell Lady Moon
She's trying
She's dying

Higher still, she floats
Above this spinning ball
This wild universe
A universe that brought our hands

Our hearts, our love
Together

A universe that let me pull
It all
Apart

No one's laughing, she tells me
Not I, Lady Moon, nor my shimmering stars
Nor the inky black sky that bleeds tears
In my shadows

But she insists
You must

Let
Him
Go

Take him from me, I beg
For my heart doesn't have the strength
To give him up

Dangling high above my head now
My moon, she loves me so
Her light opens my palms
Washes away the warmth of your touch

Her beams brush my brow
Flitter across my lashes
Over my eyes, red from loss
They shoot straight into the chest
That is holding you hostage

There is a war in there
I wonder if you even know
How bloody I've become
In this battle

Lady Moon, she knows
She knows the way you only saw me
She remembers the way we held each other
As if the next breath we shared
Could be our last

And she was there, when it really was
Our last

So she fights for me
This night
As I lie alone in my bed
My fingers tapping over letters
That have spelled out my love for you
In innumerable ways

She knows how the language of my heart
Only wants to tell the story
Of you
Of us

And yet, she fights

For me
For you
For us

So that I may truly
Let
You
Go

The battle ends in tears
In blood
In death

Everything ends like this
She reminds me
As she leaves my body
In a heap
Of missing you

When I gaze up at the stars
I notice they are
No longer
The stars that once lit your eyes
In the days when you were mine

No, they're gone

And I am here, alone
Remembering who I am
In the light of a moon
Who knows the truth
Of my battered heart

Before she disappears
Too high in the ether
For these mortal eyes to see
Another whisper...

Wait for Brother Sun, she says
It's only a few more hours now, my love
Until he kisses your sleepy eyes
And helps you to see
The glory, the beauty, the utter magnificence of this life
Now that you have finally

Let
Him
Go

Partie III

Une femme
~ A woman ~

FOR THE FIRST TIME

For the first time
I kissed the hungry lips
Of a man I barely know
And I didn't remember
The taste of yours

Soft, wet, sweet
Adoration
That twisted
Into obligation

For the first time
I lay beneath the weight
Of a man who is not you
And I didn't miss
Your strong arms

The way they held
Loved
Suffocated
Every piece
Of my dying heart

For the first time
I spread my legs for a man
Who is nothing like you

Like either of you

And I wished for him
To be inside of me
In a way neither of you ever were
Or ever could be

For the first time
Since I left you

Both of you

I didn't let a man
Ravage me
When I wanted him to

I didn't need his sex
To fill the shallow hole
Left in the absence
Of you

The way I have
For endless nights
And tiresome mornings
Since our love dissipated
Into the stars

For the first time
I slept naked, legs intertwined
With another man
And I didn't dream of you
Wanting me back

For the first time
I didn't awaken in another man's bed
Denying my tears
Denying my grief

For the first time
I watched the way the morning sun
Kissed the sleepy eyes
Of another

And I didn't wish
They were your eyes
Or your hair
Your nose
Your lips

It was only later
After I left his warm sheets
That I remembered you

Both of you

But the memory only came
For me to realize
That I did not think of you
That I did not miss you
That I did not regret
The day I left you

Either of you

For the first time
Since my wild soul
Escaped the prisons
Of our love

My heart is beating
For someone
Who is not you

For someone
Who is not
The man I slept wrapped up in
Last night

My heart is beating
For me
Only me

IN THE MEADOW

In the meadow
Where I go
Every day
When the sun is high
And I am low

I do not hear your voice
Twisted and sick
As you say to me
Sometimes it's better
To shut
The fuck
Up

After I have revealed to you
The deepest, darkest parts
Of myself
My story
My soul

In the meadow
The sweet song of the birds
The sweeping sound of the wind
The swishing laugher of the trees
Suffocates the disharmonious echoes
Of your manipulative words
And the blaring silences
Where you stared me down
Waiting for me to apologize
When I had done nothing wrong

In the meadow
I hear none of this

In the meadow
You
And your sickness
Cease to Exist

In the meadow
The song that flitters past my cheeks
And dances in my hair
Is golden and shining
With relief

Because I escaped from the hell
You would have built for us
From the way you refused to hear my words
My truth
My beauty

But instead
You wanted to control and dominate
In your nauseating, feminine voice

A man who presented himself
As something
He was so obviously not

In the meadow
Among the flowers that bloom in endless sight
Among the fields buzzing with bees and butterflies
There is a sweet death
A violent and triumphant ending
To your wretched ways

In the meadow
The rays of light that blast through my skin
And penetrate my bloody, beating heart
Could never
Hold an ounce
Of you
Or your poison
In their beauty

In the meadow
I am pure
I am cleansed
I am free

THERE WILL BE FIRE

There will be fire
A friend once told me
Anytime you are
Growing, changing, evolving
Into someone new
Someone who doesn't take
The infection of mediocrity
As the everyday hum
Of your precious life

Those who once walked by your side
Will be swallowed in flames
If they do not
Grow, change, evolve
Alongside you

They
Will
Burn

Their old words, once a soft caress
Now, crisp as toast
Your memory of their love
Will scatter like ashes
In an endless ocean of loss

There will be fire
He told me
I knew this, of course
When the hot merciless embers
Of your desire
Sizzled atop my hungry tongue

I knew this, of course
As the lost loves of a thousand men
Have threatened my flesh
For all the years I've taken up
On this fiery planet

But this is the way
We move, grow
Change, evolve
Through our precious lives

With fire and flames
With annihilation and death
Of old ways
Stale friends
Venomous loves

And so it is only
Through the hell of loss
That we emerge
To the beauty of new light
To the promise of new hope
To the glory of new love

A bright, precious life
That is born
Of destruction

So it was
In the end
The fire
Who loved me most
For without the burns

Without the loss
Of all of you

I would not be
Me

There will be fire, he said
And my lips curved
Into a grin, a dare

I'm not finished growing, I said

Mediocrity and boredom
Inauthenticity and fear
I will pour gas over your toxicity
And light a thousand matches

However many it takes
To wash clean
The black soot that has piled
Atop my beautiful heart

Bring on the flames
Bring on the loss
Bring on the pain

I said
Grinning
Standing
Welcoming
The fire

THE SILENCE OF FREEDOM

I have freed myself
From all men
From most belongings
From family obligation
From your expectation
That someday
I would get a real job

I have found what so many
Only wish
They could have

Freedom
It is not at all
What I expected it to be

Sweeter than honey
Are the moments
When I give myself
The youth we never had

Jubilance
Is what I know
In every instance
When I can do whatever
The fuck
I want

Without asking you
If my dreams, my whims, my desires
Suit your rigid life plan

Ice cream before sunrise
Sex with whomever
Whenever
I want
Tsunamis of laughter
Night binges of writing
The hilarity of smoking pot
With new boys
And kissing them, perhaps
Or not
I get to decide

And the sweetness
Of cuddling with my cats
When twilight settles in
Or when the sun rises
Just beyond the windows
Of the big house on the hill
Where I now live
With three boys

A quirky, cool life
Born of the sweetness of this freedom
I have officially claimed
As my own

In that freedom
There lives a silence
That at times
Comforts me
In ways you never could

A silence I treasure
More than chocolate and orgasms

Then there are moments
Scattered throughout my new life
Like fallen leaves
In a city that has no seasons
Moments when this silence
Brings me to my knees

Because the silence of freedom is, of course
At its essence
A never ending
Forever reminder
Of the absence
Of you

A NEW NORMAL

My new normal
Carries pieces of you
But more of me
Than ever before

My new normal
Is still learning
But so much wiser
Than the girl I used to be

My new normal
Still loves you
But loves herself more
Than the deception of romance

My new normal
Knows grief by name
But is filled with more light
Than the eyes of a million men

My new normal
Is a changed, hopeful heart
That longs to embrace another
In a brilliantly imperfect union

My new normal
Is a vibrant woman
Who lives her truth, and writes it
Like the badass she has become

My new normal
Is swiping right and swiping left

Dating up a storm, living a youth
I once chose to cut short, with the slice of a diamond

My new normal
Is the beautiful mess I was always meant to be
Dancing and writing and creating
With total and complete abandon

My new normal
Is finding a way
To move forward alone
With the grace only seen
Floating atop wispy clouds, across a dewdrop sky

My new normal
Dreams of Paris and chocolate
And handprints on steamy windows
And she no longer has to pretend to be content
With the fatally mundane routine of marriage

My new normal
Is a daily test to embrace
The wild new life I've created
In the absence of you

My new normal
Is brilliant and enchanting
Eccentric and honest
Fabulous and never ending

And me
So completely, unapologetically me

THE GEMS I WILL NOT HIDE

Strength engulfs me
And I will, no longer
Balance on tip-toes, behind the tree
Where your comfort blooms

Those blossoms are laced with poison
Not sure if you knew
But I'm finished killing myself
With their nectar

Power fills my lungs
And I will, no longer
Hold my breath, waiting for the moment
When you say I can speak

Your words have left my ears
Not sure if you knew
But I'm finished living
By your dead poetry

Beauty envelops my soul
And I will, no longer
Conceal my precious gems, in the rotting chest
Where you send glory to die

My radiance cannot be stifled
Not sure if you knew
But I'm finished letting your fear
Suffocate my insatiable zest

Light radiates through my core
And I will, no longer
Dim my glow, to live in the shadows
Of your terrified heart

My fearless heart, she shines bright
Not sure if you knew
But I'm finished shielding your eyes
From the electric spark of my love

BROKEN, I AM NOT

My heart may have shattered
My chest may have cracked
My dreams may have gone up in flames

My lungs may have ceased to breathe
And I may have considered ending it all
More times
Than I will ever admit

But what I have learned
In this insane journey to rock bottom
Is that beyond my bleeding heart and my crushed bones
Beyond the ashes of my lost dreams
And the last breath I believed I would ever take...

Lives a soul
A glorious, vibrant soul
Who is untouchable, unbreakable, indestructible
The ultimate warrior of love
Who welcomes rock bottom
Who cries victory at the sound of my broken heart

She emerges from dust and ash
Brushing off shards of broken bone
Kicking away mounds of bloody flesh
And she is smiling, triumphant, radiant
As she reminds me

You are not that lacerated flesh
You are not that scorching pain
That you so wish to cling to

You are me
I am you

And broken, I am not

NEAR THE LIGHT

Near the light she stood
Where grace had no name
She called out for it nonetheless
But just out of her reach
It sparkled, shined, bled
In her hands

Near the light she wept
Where love had once lived
She called out to him
But he didn't come
He loved, pierced, killed
Her heart

Near the light she danced
Where glory used to shine
She called out to her lost inspiration
But beyond her pointed toes
It swirled, twirled, slipped
Through her grasp

Near the light she loved
Where she once gave everything
She called out to all she had lost

Come back, come back, come back...

But in the darkness
Only echoes of her broken heart
Returned

Near the light she nearly died
Where she once stood, wept, danced, loved
She had no voice left to call out
But just before her last breath
A whisper kissed her lips

It was truth
Her truth

In that moment
Grace, glory, inspiration, and love
Breathed peace into her soul

We were here all along, they said
All you had to do
Was step
Into the light

Her eyes opened
And she saw
Life
Where there had been none

Full, unending, new

Beautiful

She stood
In the light
Of her truth

START AGAIN

One day, you look up
And no longer does it hurt
To gaze straight into the light
Of a blazing sun
Or feel its heat
Sizzling on your fair skin

One day, you smile
And no longer does it feel
Like a forced moment, a fake laugh
No, this time your lips are curving upward
Into an exquisite dance of truth
Upon your shining face

One day, your heart beats faster
And no longer does it feel
Like a blade has carved out the good parts
And left you for dead
Instead, this beating drum is so very alive
So very full of love
Not for the ones who broke your heart
Or for the others who shattered it

But for yourself

For the choices you've made
For the ways in which you've saved yourself
For the times when you thought you couldn't go another day
But you did

You woke up, you stood up, you breathed
Sunrise into sunset...
Even when you couldn't bear to look at the light
All through the night...
Even when you couldn't sleep without a pill
And then again, at dawn...
When the memories assaulted you
Before you'd even set one foot on the ground

Through all of that, you persevered
You kept going

And now, here you are
A beautiful being of strength
Bathing in the sunlight
Smiling as a heartbeat...your heartbeat
Sings a song only you can hear

You survived, she sings
The darkness is behind you, she whispers
You no longer belong to the past, she breathes

You're here
You're now
You're alive

Now go
Fearlessly
Into this wild world
And start again, my love...
Start again

MY WISH FOR YOU, DEAR READER

May you love truly so that you may know true loss
May you lose so that you break open
May you be broken so that your light seeps in

May your light shatter the darkness

And in its place, may you rediscover
The unending source of love
That has always existed within you

May you blossom in this love
In your own unique way

And trust, in your heart
That where there is love
Wounds are healed
The lost are found
And dreams—even your wildest—come true

May you not fear loss, dear reader

For within that loss
Lies your greatest power
Your greatest strength

Your source
Your love
Your light
Your truth

Within that loss
Lies the greatest gift
This Universe has ever known:

You

READ ON FOR AN EXCERPT
FROM THE MEMOIR THAT INSPIRED THE POEMS:

*P*MEET ME IN
Paris
A MEMOIR

AVAILABLE IN
PAPERBACK & EBOOK

Le Prologue

No matter the season, no matter the weather, love is *always* in the air in Paris.

And tonight is no different.

The autumn sun has been swept away by a splattering of gray clouds, blanketing the city's cobblestone streets in one of those inky, mysterious Parisian nights where lovers' secrets will be swept away by the choppy waters of the Seine, or captured whole by the Gothic towers of Notre Dame, or better yet, swallowed up by the bottle of red wine my own lover and I are sharing in a charming little bar near Châtelet.

Yes, I've taken a lover.

In Paris.

A Paris lover.

Oh, how I adore the taste of those delicious words.

The Merlot slips past my lips, smooth and rich, as I smile at this most disarming man I have by my side. I give him a look that is both coy and inviting, in lust and falling—well, more like plummeting—headfirst and harder than ever before.

It is only the third time we've been together, and already, this lover of mine has hopped on a plane from Chicago to spend a few days with me in Paris.

I'm not sure if he understands how much his presence by my side, in my beloved city, means to me. Or how each touch of his strong hands, each adoring smile, each endearing tilt of his head is healing this broken heart of mine.

Divorce has a way of shattering hearts like nothing else. And mine is no exception. It has only been a few months since I left my husband—the man I have loved for twelve years, the man I still love, despite my choice to leave our dying marriage—and I know these days in Paris with my lover will be my only happy ones for some time.

We've spent this crisp fall day strolling hand in hand along the hilly streets of Montmartre, devouring *croissants aux amandes* and *pains au chocolat*, stealing kisses in abandoned courtyards, sipping espresso at hilltop cafés, flirting with every word, every breath, and falling ever so hopelessly in love.

Although neither of us wants to admit it yet.

As my lover drinks his wine, he gives me a sly look that says, *Get up, go to the bathroom, let me slip off your jeans, and I'll take you right here, right now.*

I haven't known him that long, but I know what his looks mean.

"We're only a few blocks from our flat in the Marais," I say to this insatiable man. "And besides, French bathrooms are *so* tiny."

"That's a few blocks too far," he replies, sliding his hand up my thigh. "And *you're* so tiny. I think we'll be just fine."

"*Lover.* You'll just have to wait." I smack his hand, loving the way he wants me so.

The truth is, in the days since I left my marriage, I've been ravenous for affection, for sex, for love. A lioness let out of her cage. Raw, powerful, and in need.

I would let my lover take me anytime, anywhere. And he knows it.

But I *so* enjoy teasing him.

Suddenly my older, playful lover becomes all serious, taking my hand.

A long silence stretches between us as he holds my gaze. I have a feeling that whatever is coming will probably make me cry.

Finally, he speaks.

"No matter what happens with us in the future, whether you're finished with me after Paris or we can't stay away from each other for the rest of our lives, promise me...*promise me*...that at some point in the next five years, we'll meet again in Paris."

I glance down at my lover's silver wedding band, not meaning to, not wanting to, but my eyes go there, if only to remind myself of the reality of our situation. That I am falling in love with a man who is mine and who isn't mine. A man who is healing my heart and ripping it apart, all at the same time.

I can't stop the tears from rimming my eyes as I look up into his intense green gaze, the gaze that unhinges me completely, unravels my heart, makes me do all sorts of things I never would have dreamt of doing before he stormed into my life.

Or before *I* stormed into *his*.

It is here, lost in his eyes, where I forget all about my wounded heart.

"Hmm. Me, you, Paris, in the next five years..." I hesitate, pretending to consider my options.

"Promise me," he demands as he squeezes my waist and pulls me close so he can run those deadly lips of his along my neck.

He can't get enough of me; since the day I met him, he never could.

"Yes. I promise," I whisper, once I've caught my breath.

And then his lips find mine in this bar in Paris, where no one knows us, where no one recognizes the romance writer and her lover, holding on to each other, making promises we aren't sure we can keep, but making them all the same.

When we dash out of the bar moments later, 1 wonder how many secrets the wind is carrying as it whips past, waltzing over cobblestones, rustling through trees.

Quite a lot, 1 imagine, in a city this grand, a city this thrilling, a city so gloriously full of love.

A NOTE OF THANKS

I am truly grateful for the inspiration that has come to me each time I've found myself at the keyboard, weaving words together to create a new poem. While these words are my own, while they have poured from my heart through my fingertips and onto this page, I am aware that there is something much greater at work in these moments of inspiration and creation, and I am honored to be part of such a beautiful process.

ABOUT THE AUTHOR

Juliette Sobanet is the award-winning author of five Paris-based romance and mystery novels, four short stories, and her new memoir, *Meet Me in Paris*. Her books have hit the Top 100 Bestseller Lists on Amazon US, UK, Germany, and France, and her work has been published in Italian, Romanian, and Turkish, with more on the way. A former French professor, Juliette holds a B.A. from Georgetown University and an M.A. from New York University in Paris. She is a blogger for *The Huffington Post*, and she writes about her personal experience with divorce on her blog, *Confessions of a Romance Novelist*. Juliette is currently planning her move to France, where she will fulfill her dream of writing full-time while devouring chocolate croissants every morning and sipping wine at sidewalk cafés every evening.

I Loved You in Paris is her first book of poetry.

Visit Juliette's website at
www.juliettesobanet.com

www.ingramcontent.com/pod-product-compliance
Lightning Source LLC
LaVergne TN
LVHW041324080426
835513LV00008B/581